A CROMER MISCELLANY

Further details of Poppyland Publishing titles can be found at
www.poppyland.co.uk
where clicking on the 'Support and Resources' button will lead to pages
specially compiled to support this title.

POPPYLAND
PUBLISHING

For Mum and Dad

A CROMER MISCELLANY

Adrian Vicary

Picture Credits:

All pictures from the collection of, or taken by, Philip or Adrian Vicary, unless otherwise attributed in the caption.

Preface

Adrian Vicary's introduction on page 7 gives us the background to this remarkable book. Much of the work done by his father to make copy photographs from earlier prints has enabled us to still be able to access these images; otherwise they would have disappeared years ago. These pictures have often been used in other books over the decades but it is right that they are brought together in this collection.

Philip and his family kept Westward Ho! hotel – see pages 17-19 – but throughout he maintained the recording of the famous and the routine in the town. Of the day of the *Sepoy* rescue in 1933 – see pages 49-54 – he recalled how he had heard the maroons, at that time fired to summon the lifeboat crew, and had made his way to the east beach. He found a position on the cliff where he could get a little shelter in order to manage his camera and precious plates and then recorded the events of that dramatic 13th December. Every shot needed the plate in the camera to be changed by fingers numbed with cold, but he stuck at the task throughout the day as the *Sepoy* dragged her anchor, bumped over the breakwater and started to break up in front of him. With the crew finally rescued as Coxswain Henry Blogg brought the motor lifeboat *H.F.Bailey* back from a service much further round the coast, his task was not over. He had to get the plates off to the evening train to London, the result being a full page photograph on the front of the next day's *Daily Mirror*, and various other publications making use of his pictures.

He arranged for the crew to come down to the beach the next day so that he could get them all in a photo – see page 53 – only to have a national photographer arrive, say, 'That's just what I wanted' – and take advantage of Philip's organising. Ah, well, the real scoop was the previous day.

In our age of camera phones and instant transfer of pictures, he takes us back to the adventure of obtaining such pictures. Alongside are the perhaps more straightforward but equally evocative images of steam locomotives in the Cromer stations, the mundane photos of the gasworks that no-one else bothered to record, the detailed images from the top of the church tower which provide us with timelines of development – just some of the pictures we can enjoy in this book.

PJRS
Sept 2017

The west end of Church Street photographed from the Fiveways or Crossways about 1959. On the left is 'Green and Grey coaches' booking office. In the centre is Cox's fishmongers and, on the right, Gibson's butchers and greengrocers with their painted advertisement on the projecting wall.

Also on the right is Baxter's, again a butchers, and still a butcher's shop as we write in 2017.

The shops on the left of the 'Narrows' were all demolished in 1963, to provide a wider pavement and road.

Bibliography

Many books were consulted in the preparation of this selection but particular mention must be made of the following:

Savin, A.C., *History of Cromer,* Rounce & Wortley, 1950 edition.
Stibbons, Brenda & Peter, *A Cromer Album,* Poppyland Publishing 1985
Warren, Martin, *Around Cromer* Alan Sutton 1995
Pipe, Christopher, *The Story of Cromer Pier,* Poppyland Publishing 1998
Pipe, Christopher, *A Dictionary of Cromer & Overstrand History,* Poppyland Publishing 2010

Cromer –An Historical Miscellany

Many books have been published over the years dealing with Cromer and its history in different ways. No pictorial assortment like this one can pretend to be comprehensive, nor is it the first of its kind. What has been attempted is to make a collection which, I hope, can be enjoyed on its own and, at the same time, introduce new material which adds something to what has gone before. The contents come from the collection of my late father, Philip Vicary. The nineteenth century photographs were collected by him over many years from various friends and, while some will be familiar from previous appearances, I think they deserve another look. Most of the twentieth century photographs, post 1910, were taken by my father, with a small number from other family members. He was privileged to be a friend of Henry Blogg and this made it possible to record some more relaxed shots of Henry than were usually seen. These have been included for the first time here.

The contents begin with the nineteenth century and start in the east swinging round through the south to the west to show the town in its setting as it developed. Then follows the front of the town and the beach in the same period. The rest is made up of various twentieth century subjects of diverse nature which have either not been included in previous books or are looked at anew, particularly in the case of the wreck of the *Sepoy*. In the captions I have tried to give a guide to what can be seen and then leave it to the picture itself to 'speak' to the viewer. I am, like others, grateful to the cameramen (and lithographers) who worked in the nineteenth century for providing so many fine pictures which we can enjoy still.

I must also record my grateful thanks to Tony for details of the family connection with A.J.Rogers' studio and to Peter for enthusiastically accepting the book and his patience and expertise in preparing it for publication.

Adrian Vicary 2017

1 Happy Valley depicted in an 1831 lithograph. The land belonged to the manor of Overstrand and, as is evident, was used to graze cattle. Prominent in the view is Cromer lighthouse, originally built in 1719 and first lit on 29th September that year by means of a coal fire in an iron grate. The building was modified in 1792 with a better light provided by a cluster of five oil lamps backed by reflectors and made to rotate, thus presenting a single identifying flash every minute. Falls brought the cliff edge closer to the lighthouse and a large fall in 1832 prompted the decision by Trinity House to erect a new tower four hundred yards further back. This was first lit on 29th June 1833 and, with periodical modifications, is still operating today. The old lighthouse was abandoned and was finally carried away in another cliff fall in 1866.

Cromer itself can be seen as a small cluster of houses around the church but Colne House is shown as the first outward development to the south. Also discernible, just below the distant Beeston Bump, is the windmill which may be seen again in picture 8 and on page 14.

2 A similar view, further forward in the valley c.1895 showing the first clubhouse of the Royal Cromer Golf Club. In the expanding town some of the major buildings shown are Newhaven Court on the left in front of the woods on Arbor Hill; the Grand Hotel, to the left of the church tower; the Hotel de Paris with its central dome and the Jetty. The Sugar Loaf is prominent to the right of centre with the Warren Woods adjacent.

3   The east cliff path in 1886. On the left, in front of the church, is North Lodge; then the Coastguard watch house (the white building); just to the right of that, on the curve of the Crescent, the houses are still only two storeys in height. No Hotel de Paris is visible as yet and the Jetty has its six outer supports cross-braced. On the beach are two of the collier schooners, *Ellis* and *Commerce*.

4   Ten years later and the east cliff path is now enclosed between iron railings. North Lodge has been extended, the buildings on the Crescent raised in height, the Hotel de Paris completely rebuilt and the three outermost Jetty supports replaced by ones made of iron. Now there are no colliers.

5   The buildings are much the same about two years later but the Jetty
     has gone after being severely damaged in a storm in November
     1897. This storm also damaged the roof of Beach House which is the
     prominent light-coloured building at promenade level – compare the
     flat roof here with the two previous pictures. In the foreground is the
     Doctor's Steps zig-zag slope to the Promenade with access provided to
     the upper floor of the shelter.

6   The church and Vicarage as seen from Arbor Hill in about 1870. This
     date is assumed from the well-established state of the garden, the
     Vicarage having been built in 1854. It is interesting that the drive is
     fenced in front of and to the right of the house which suggests that the
     grassed area was used for grazing.

7   A similar viewpoint perhaps fifteen years later with the chancel and
     aisles of the church not yet rebuilt. Buildings have been completed on
     the south side of Church Street, notably obscuring the south porch of
     the church. The Vicarage's grass now looks as if it has become a lawn
     and the trees have grown as high as the roof. Across the foreground

is the kitchen garden wall belonging to Newhaven Court. South facing, it has upright and fan-trained fruit trees against it. It would be interesting to know how well they did; what price peaches, nectarines or apricots?

8   A watercolour sketch of Cromer from the south-west – with allowance
         made for the, unknown, artist's licence – in the 1830s. It is of interest
         for the view of the mill, clearly a post mill with its timber trestle
         supports open to the elements and with a pole to turn the body into
         the wind. This type of mill had been in existence in Britain since the
         fourteenth century. This one was probably the last mill to work in
         Cromer.

9   An 1831 lithograph of Cromer from the west cliff with the 1821-built
         Jetty clearly shown. Interestingly, the landward end, which is carried
         over a solidly built substructure, is barely above the level of the steeply
         shelving beach. The outer part was supported on cast iron legs and
         brackets. Also to be noted is that there is no sea wall or any form of
         revetment to protect the base of the cliffs in front of the town.

10   The west cliff in about 1880 before the westward developments began
         to proceed up the hill. The narrowness of the Runton Road is evident
         as it lies between the timber post-and-rail fence and the white painted
         flint wall beyond.

11   A fine panorama from 1883 with the first house of what, over the next few years, would become the Marlborough Hotel on the corner of New Street and Prince of Wales Road. The first section of the western promenade is complete with its return wall just below Melbourne House. The 'new' lighthouse is now 50 years old.

12   The Marlborough now has its first extension southwards. On the Runton Road, the flint wall has been replaced by a neat stepped low brick wall with cast iron railings between short pyramidal-capped pillars. This view can be dated c.1889 since the roof of the new chancel of the church can be seen.

13   From further up the cliff the buildings on the west side of Prince of
      Wales Road are revealed. The five on the right, arranged with each
      being a mirror-image of the next, were the first to be built on this side
      of the road in 1885/6. The two-bay building in flint and brick, standing
      apart, was the first section of what would be Westward Ho! Built in
      1890, the same year that the Jetty had its three outermost supports
      replaced with iron ones.

14   The foreground is dominated by the new Grand Hotel completed in
      1891. The other major development is the complete remodelling of
      the Marlborough, now with two matching wings joined by a central
      onion-domed turret. The date of this photograph must be c.1895 since
      also visible is the dome of the newly rebuilt Hotel de Paris, above the
      left end of the Marlborough.

15   Here we have the booklet produced in the 1930s to send to prospective customers in which details of the hotel's accommodation and prices were given, together with notes suggesting what might be of interest in the town and local area. The photograph of the back of the hotel can be compared with photo 13. The next section to be built filled the gap between the two existing buildings and finally the two-bay section on the seaward end completed the hotel. This last section was in flint and brick to match the original. The whole was finished c.1898. Later the first of the five original houses to the south was purchased and became part of Westward Ho!

Although no notable names were recorded in the visitors' book, the people who did come seem to have been happy with their stay, since there were no stories of serious discontent. The worst that could be remembered was the occasion on which one lady guest said to her companion at dinner that the shepherd's pie was "Nothing but a Monday makeshift"! Neither were there any major upsets in the running of the hotel except, perhaps, for the occasion in August 1912 when prolonged heavy rain caused flooding of the semi-basements and areas, necessitating a visit from Cromer's horse-drawn steam fire engine to pump the water out.

After the Second World War trade did not recover to its pre-war level. Tastes altered and the general difficulties of the time led to a change in holiday styles and choice of accommodation. After the 1956 season, the doors were closed for the last time and the hotel and contents sold.

WESTWARD HO! HOTEL
CROMER

CROMER FROM THE EAST CLIFF

FRONT VIEW OF HOTEL.

VIEW OF HOTEL FROM TENNIS COURTS.

ENTRANCE HALL AND LOUNGE.

TEA LOUNGE

Westward Ho!

HOURS OF MEALS.

Weekdays		Sundays	
Breakfast	- 9.0 a.m.	Breakfast	- 9.0 a.m.
Luncheon	- 1.15 p.m.	Dinner	- 1.30 p.m.
Afternoon Tea	4 to 4.30 p.m.	Tea	- 5.0 p.m.
Dinner	- 7.0 p.m.	Supper	- 8.0 p.m.
Coffee			

VALUABLES. The Proprietors will not be responsible for articles of value unless handed in at the office, and a receipt taken for them.

DOGS are not allowed in the public rooms, and are charged 2/- per day.

Westward Ho!

TARIFF (inclusive).

Board and Residence.

April, May and June	3 and 3½ guineas per week each person.		
July	- 3½, 4 to 4½	,,	,,
August	- 4, 4½ to 5½	,,	,,
September	3½ 4 to 4½	,,	,,

(according to size and position of room).

Extras.

Early Morning Tea	-	- each person	6d. (per pot)
Meals in Bedroom	-	- ,,	6d.
Gas Fires in Bedrooms	-	-	

16   This very well known view along Church Street, taken around 1870, is included for two reasons. It is a superb picture, taken in the afternoon during early or late summer, with the high sun giving perfect lighting to give depth to the composition and the detail of the buildings in shadow being revealed by reflected light from those opposite. Secondly, it also makes an interesting comparison with the next photograph.

17   About the same time of day but further eastwards along the street; the date is said to be 1889 and this is probably about right as the intervening years have allowed the architectural changes here shown to have been carried out. Comparison shows that some houses have been completely rebuilt while others have been modified. The fundamental change is on the north side – i.e. south facing – where nearly every house has one or more bay windows. It seems that everyone wanted them and was able to afford to have the work done! Today there is some misunderstanding about the purpose of such windows, it being suggested that they were to provide a seat with a view. More importantly, they increased the size of a room to which they were added and allowed in more light from their greater area of glazing.

The composition of this photo is less good aesthetically but it has fine detail and clarity. Also interesting is the sandy earth road surface which must have been unpleasant in wet weather.

18   Garden Street about 1877. Although this has appeared in print before
     it is worth inclusion for another look. Mainly of interest are the
     characters shown. There are eight boys, aged about five to ten; note the
     one on the left holding on firmly to his dog and the others displaying
     variations of that problem of what to do with the hands – down by
     the side; clasped behind the back; hands on hips. The man on the left,
     thumbs in his belt, looks a tough customer and the one right of centre
     has a hand in a pocket. The bearded gent. in the door of the shop,
     hand on heart, is possibly William Lake, corn chandler. The elderly
     lady at her front door might be Mrs Clarke. Note the cobbled surface
     in the gutter. Further down the street are two ladies, one cleaning the
     windows, and a little girl. Everyone is aware of the cameraman. There
     is a horse and cart at the bottom of the street with the sea beyond, if
     you could but see it.

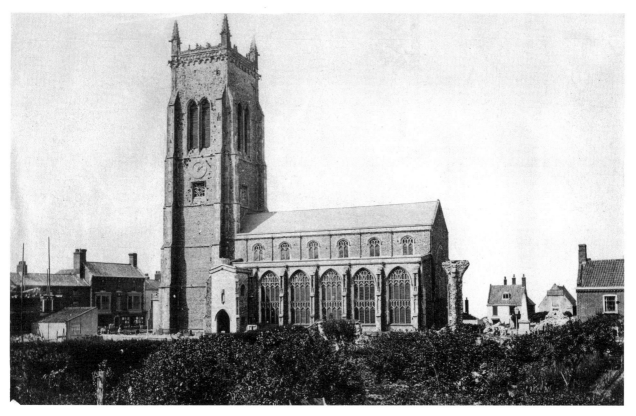

19 The parish church in about 1882. The chancel had been missing for 200 years. The only piece of masonry still standing was one pier from between the two windows of the eastern end of the south aisle. No chancel allows a good view of Ditchell's house and former granary beyond. At that date the granary was in use as stables.

20 From about the same date comes this view inside the nave looking towards the curtained blank east wall. Note the position of the font in the centre of the cross aisle from the south porch. Two interested gentlemen are studying it closely, something which needed one foot on a hassock apparently?

PART OF CROMER PREMISES.

21   To mark the 150th Anniversary of the company, Rusts Ltd. produced
      a commemorative booklet. As well as a brief history of the shop,
      its development and some notes about the family, it contains some
      interesting photographs. On the right the 1870 view at the top shows
      the premises at the top of High Street as seen from within the north-
      west corner of the churchyard. The booklet's text records that "…
      in 1892 the shop front was smashed by a runaway horse and cab,
      which starting from the 'Red Lion' cliff, came along the street and
      overturned, on account of the speed, in attempting to turn down High
      Street." The whole property shown was rebuilt and expanded, from
      1896, into the form still recognisable, above the shop fronts, today.
      This is shown, in part, in the next photograph of the then current
      fleet of delivery vans lined up outside. It is amusing to note that the
      telephone number was 9!

RUSTS IN 1870.

THE RISE OF RUSTS.

" Prepare th.y work without; and make it fit for thyself in the field, and afterwards build thine house."—Proverbs ch. 24 v. 27.

WHEN Benjamin Rust first opened his tiny shop in High Street, Cromer, 150 years ago, he had just finished his apprenticeship of seven years, with William Daniels, a grocer and tallow chandler, at Yarmouth. He had taken over a general business which had already been in existence for many years, but it is most unlikely that the youth ever thought that he was destined to be the Founder of a business concern which would grow and progress until it became a Departmental Store employing 100 persons, and occupying a pre-eminent position in the leading seaside resort of North Norfolk.

Benjamin Rust was born in 1758, the son of a yeoman farmer and landowner at Palling, and he commenced his apprenticeship in the grocery trade in 1771, ending it in 1778. Cromer was then but a decayed coast town, with a population of under 700 souls, and it is not known what made him decide to venture to set up in business for himself in the town; but he appears to have taken a lease of a shop which was one of a row of ten owned by a James Kirby.

Benjamin was undoubtedly a man " diligent in business " for on July 5th, 1798, he was able to buy this shop, and six others for the sum of £550. The present Grocery Department of Rusts

PAGE THREE

FLEET OF DELIVERY VANS.

22   Jetty Street around the turn of the 20th century. The horse and cart,
well laden, is standing outside Russell House which, for many years,
was a bakery – so perhaps it was waiting to set off on a delivery round.
The tea room was at Number 5.

23 An engraving by G. Pank dated 1821 of the newly erected Jetty. If the depiction of the structure is anywhere near accurate, it was a curious one, with a breakwater apparently under the centre of it. One suspects a strong artistic licence here and that the 1831 lithograph on p. 14 probably gives a better idea of its actual appearance. Nevertheless the engraving has a naïve charm which makes it appealing.

24 The new Jetty, completed in 1846, appears in this beautiful lithograph from 1854, as does the sea wall protecting the west cliff. The figures are interesting with fishermen sorting their catch in the foreground, ladies and children walking on the beach, a rider exercising his horse (did he take it into the sea?); but what is being carried by the man with a pole over his right shoulder – seaweed? On the left, just in the waves, are two bathing machines. On the skyline, the lighthouse of 1833 can be seen above the Jetty and the tower of the earlier one to the left.

25   On the east beach c.1891 with the seaward end of the Jetty on its three
      sets of cast iron legs and the new Red Lion (seen between Beach House
      and the church) completed in 1887. There is much industrious activity
      by the children and some are looking after a pair of goat-carts, one
      two-wheeled and one four-wheeled. There are no bathing machines in
      view so they might all be on duty, out of shot to the right.

26   Chairs for the sands and bathing machines in action, with many more
      waiting for custom. The lady in the foreground is using an upturned
      basket as the base for a writing desk. The date of this photo must be
      c.1896/7; the Metropole, centre of the picture, has been built (1893)
      and the Hotel de Paris rebuilt (1895) but the Jetty is still there – it was
      to be destroyed in November 1897 together with the pitched roof of
      Beach House.

27   An early morning picture, also c.1891. The bathing machines are lined up
      with a horse standing by for duty and two boats are drying their sails. In
      the middle of the photo, the flights of steps down to the promenade from
      the Red Lion have had their retaining walls freshly painted and the hotel's
      name prominently painted up.

28   A photograph full of atmosphere, taken from the Crescent, on what looks
      like a hot day. There was very little wind because the white ensign at the
      Coastguard station is hanging limply. There are plenty of takers for the
      bathing machines judging by those visible jostling for space at the edge
      of the sea. Mr. Miller was the proprietor of the bathing machines and
      his board can be seen propped against the pole at the foot of the lifeboat
      slipway. That pole is one of several supporting drying lines for bathing
      costumes.

29   The main interest in this photograph, which gives a good view of
Beach House with its flat roof, put on after the 1897 storm, is that it
shows the ticket office for the bathing machines now in the care of
Mr. J. Davies. As can be seen, tickets cost five shillings for a dozen,
single bath [sic] sixpence. A separate board, hanging on the side
between the wheels, states 'swimming lessons given'.

30   The schooner *Wensleydale* was owned by Mr. Jeremiah Cross, coal
merchant, of Cromer and Overstrand. After his death in 1878 the ship
was sold. Here seen in 1872, she has brought in a cargo of coal, though
there is little sign of activity. A coal cart is going up the Gangway
so perhaps unloading had been completed and she is waiting for the
next tide. The line to her kedge anchor can be seen running across
the beach in the foreground. As soon as she was afloat she would haul
herself off and recover her anchor.

31 An ink and pencil sketch by Philip Vicary of a schooner off Cromer.
She is shown having hauled herself off after unloading and is in ballast
and making sail to depart. Up until the early years of the nineteenth
century return cargoes, mainly grain, were carried but, after the
agricultural depression of the 1830s, this trade ceased. However,
coal continued to be brought to the beach until 1887. In that year the
Eastern & Midland Railway arrived at the new Beach station. The
E&MR (and its successor, the M&GN) was ideally placed in relation to
the coalfields of the midlands and north to bring coal to Cromer (and
elsewhere in Norfolk), whereas the GER, which had arrived in Cromer
ten years earlier, was not. Therefore for those ten years it was still
necessary to bring coal by sea to meet the demand.

32 On the Jetty in the 1870s looking up at the town. On the left is Ditchell's house and barn and the church is without its chancel. In the centre is the end of Jetty Street with Victoria House facing the sea and then the Hotel de Paris dominating the scene. On the right is the back of the Belle Vue Hotel which had its frontage on High Street. The slopes down to the promenade start at the centre of Jetty Cliff with the cliff face to the west grass covered. Through the rail of the Jetty, on the east side, the flight of steps can be seen leading from the promenade to the beach. Note the continuous bench seats running the length of the Jetty on both sides. The solitary gentleman sitting there was perhaps accompanying the cameraman to provide a focal point for the picture. And lastly it is possibly out of season as only three other people are in view. It was obviously a cloudy day.

33 A similar view, this time from a few paces to the left, and now a lady
provides the focal point but back to camera! There is another lady at
the promenade end of the Jetty but otherwise, again, only three other
people. It is early morning with the low sun casting long shadows
and the date must be 1895 to 1897. The Hotel de Paris rebuilding was
completed in the former year and the Jetty destroyed in the latter.
The hotel dominates the scene even more; additionally the slopes
have been entirely rearranged, now starting from both ends of Jetty
Cliff. Apart from the fact that Cromer Pier was built further to the
right (westwards), this scene remains much the same today, the only
difference being that the bandstand at the centre of the slopes is no
longer there.

34   Regatta Day at Cromer in the 1880s. Off the end of the Jetty is the paddle vessel *Victoria*. She was a Great Yarmouth tug which, during the summer months, was sometimes used to take passengers for pleasure trips from Yarmouth harbour along the coast. At Cromer the passengers would disembark into local fishing boats to be ferried ashore to enjoy a few hours in the town. On the beach to the right are the portable landing stages used to allow the visitors to come ashore without getting their feet wet. It was on such an occasion as this that *Victoria* met with an accident. On 9th August 1888, around 3.15pm, she had just got underway with her 100 passengers to return to Yarmouth when she struck something underwater and was holed on the port side and held fast on the obstruction. This object was believed to be a substantial block of masonry from the former Shipden church, inundated in the mid-fourteenth century. It was known locally as the Church Rock. As is well known, there is no rock in north Norfolk other than chalk so it is by no means unlikely that this was a mass of flint-work from what must have been the largest building in Shipden. The tug did not sink and all the passengers were brought ashore safely by the ship's own boat and those of the local fishermen. They returned home by train. Despite trying to the free the vessel, all attempts at salvage failed and her wreck was eventually blown up, an action which also broke up the 'rock'.

35   After the loss of the Jetty in 1897, discussions began on the
      construction of a replacement, and of what form it should take.
      The engineers engaged were Douglass and Arnott and a design was
      produced and agreed upon in 1898. The necessary Parliamentary
      Bill was passed and it received Royal Assent on 9th August 1899.
      Construction was underway throughout 1900 and completed in
      1901. On 7th June 1901 the Pier was opened by Lord Claud Hamilton,
      Chairman of the Great Eastern Railway. The gates were opened with a
      gold key. This is the scene on that day at around 1.30pm.

36   A few days later and an unobstructed view shows the entrance kiosks
      with turnstiles each side of them.

37   Having negotiated the turnstiles, a jolly group of young ladies set out to tread the boards, having paid their one penny each.

38   The attractions of the day are prominently displayed on the centre gates in this photo taken in August l913. They would be performing in the pavilion theatre, which was created in 1905 by adapting the earlier open seating area with shelters and bandstand.

39   Cromer Coastguard station c.1870 showing the six men at attention
under the watchful eye of their Chief Officer. All were proficient with
their rifles and had frequent firing practices. They also manned a six-
oared cutter for rowing and sailing practice and would visit ships if
required. The men were preventive officers who patrolled the cliffs and
beaches on the lookout for smugglers and smuggling.

40   The Coastguard station in about 1914, still in the same place. With
north cone hoisted, a gale is imminent and the white ensign is already
streaming out in the strong wind. Coastguard officers were less likely
to be after smugglers at this date but were primarily looking after
the safety of shipping with visual signals like the north cone here. If
the worst happened the lifeboat could be launched, summoned by
maroons fired from the brass mortar, the barrel of which can just be
seen in the centre at the bottom of the picture.

41   Looking east from the church tower in 1885, the lower half of the
      picture shows the jumble of roofs of the buildings between the
      churchyard and the gangway. Beyond is North Lodge with its gardens
      and then Cliff House on the Overstrand Road.

42   This matching view in September 1964, when compared with the
previous photograph, shows that this one was taken from a higher
angle. The most likely explanation is that in 1885 the cameraman was
standing on the scaffolding which had been erected for the church
tower restoration that year. The changes to the buildings on and
around Brook Street can be seen – and those which have stayed much
the same. Beyond, from this higher angle, the Watch House (formerly
the Coastguard station) can be seen and, next to it, the bowling green.
The latter is part of North Lodge Park, by then owned by the Council,
with the house being the Cromer Urban District Council offices.
Other attractions provided were hard-court tennis, putting greens
and clock golf. Prominent in the centre is the roof of the workshop
belonging to the East Coast Garage with the offices, showroom and
forecourt to its right on Church Street. Cliff House is now an hotel,
to the left of which is Cliff Drive which served a 1930s housing
development.

43   Another photo taken from the scaffolding, this time looking south west. Particularly of interest is the Holt Road climbing the hill beyond the buildings on West Street. Where the road levels off at the top of the hill, just visible to the right, is the chapel of the town cemetery, opened in 1860 when the churchyard had no space left for further burials. In the fields adjacent there is, as yet, no sign of work on excavations for the approaching railway.

44   In the September 1964 comparison the railway is well shown. The
old cemetery chapel is still visible and in front of it is the station
approach forming a distinctive V-shape with the Holt Road. The Beach
station building with its platform canopy and the platform beyond
can be seen and, to its right, the goods yard and engine shed. In the
foreground, on the left is the telephone exchange, built in 1936, and
then the Meadow car park. At the bottom centre is the Parish Hall
of 1902 and in the right hand corner, the Fiveways with its central
signpost. Returning to the top of the picture, in the misty distance,
next to the railway cutting, can be seen a tall, smoking chimney which
belonged to the refuse incinerator.

45 & 46 An unprepossessing building, perhaps, but one which served
a useful purpose for more than fifty years, this is the incinerator
referred to on the previous page. It was built in Sandy Lane in 1912.
Inside the shed was a furnace into which the town's collected refuse
was shovelled to be reduced to ash. Note that the chimney stood
apart with the low-level flue passing out of the shed to the base of the
chimney. By 1974, when these photos were taken, the building was
derelict. The refuse which Cromer's expanding population produced
probably exceeded the amount it could efficiently destroy and brought
about its closure. Also, the increasing amount of plastic in the rubbish
would have created noxious fumes when burnt and, even with a tall
chimney, would have become a nuisance to the town. The result was
that rubbish was compacted and dumped in convenient 'holes' which
were covered over with earth and landscaped when full.

47 At the end of Sandy Lane was the Cromer gasworks which opened
in 1900, succeeding the previous site in Mill Road. Coal was brought
in by rail to a private siding on site. This photo also dates from 1974.
While the gasometers were still in use, the buildings which produced
and purified the gas were lying derelict. On the right was the retort
house with its roof ventilator. Here the coal was heated (not burnt) to
produce the gas in a process known as distillation. As well as the gas,
mixed with it were many impurities which had to be removed and
this would have been done in the other buildings and the cleaned gas
passed into the holders for distribution in the town's mains. This went
on until the 1950s when gas was produced by other methods elsewhere
and piped to the site for storage and distribution. This in turn was
superseded at the end of 1968 when North Sea gas was introduced.
Finally natural gas distribution was made without the need for storage
locally and the site was closed. Subsequently it was adapted for the
Anglian Water sewage treatment plant which was built in the
mid-1990s.

48   The beginnings of railway enthusiasm; armed with a box-camera
"with a piece of glass for a lens", my father, aged nine, exposed two
precious frames on what was to become a lifelong favourite: Midland
& Great Northern Joint Railway 4-4-2T Class 'A Tank' No. 9 at
Cromer Beach station.

49   Completed at Melton Constable works in March 1910, the locomotive is
here only a few months old. The yellow-brown livery is darkened by the
orthochromatic film but the gold lettering on the side tanks stands out
as does the number on the vermilion buffer beam. (The finger prints and
blotches are evidence of over-enthusiasm in the darkroom!).

50 Three years later, and with a better camera, we are now on Cromer's first station, that belonging to the Great Eastern Railway. Owing to the town nestling in a hollow with the Holt-Cromer ridge to the south and east, it was impossible for the station to be sited nearer than a mile from the town centre. With Suffield Park below and the 160 foot tower of Cromer church just visible behind the tender, No. 1850 has just come off the turntable. This was the first of the Claud Hamilton 4-4-0s to have a Belpaire firebox fitted from new, changing the GER class to D56 from the previous S46 with the round top boiler. Emerging from Stratford works in December 1903, the engine was nearing ten years old when photographed. Note the cast GER 'heraldic' device on the leading driving wheel splasher and the weeds on the platform in the foreground … disgraceful.

51   Only a few days away from the outbreak of war and weeks old, having been completed at Stratford
      in June 1914, S69 or 1500 class 4-6-0 No. 1525 simmers outside the engine shed, awaiting the return
      trip to Liverpool Street. The square top to the shed was a water tank occupying half its length with
      a pitched slated roof with ridge ventilator beyond. Kindly drivers would sometimes invite Dad up
      to the cab, endangering the white flannels which were essential wear in summer in those days – but
      parental wrath seems to have been avoided by good luck!

52   Passenger services to and from Cromer High ceased in September 1954; twenty years later the site was yet to be redeveloped with a proposed housing estate. The platforms were still in-situ and young trees had colonised the track-bed up by the buffer-stops.

53   This photo shows the locomotive inspection pit which was between the rails leading to the turntable, the site of which is in the background. The church tower can be seen above the curving wall which bordered the turntable, beside the station approach road climbing from the Suffield Park side.

54   In November 1932 at the Parish Hall, Mrs Bond Cabbell presented lifeboat
Coxswain Henry Blogg with the Silver Medal of the Royal National
Lifeboat Institution, awarded for the *Monte Nevoso* rescue of 14th to 16th
October 1932.

There have been several accounts, differing in detail, concerning the events
of the *Sepoy* wreck and rescue. A good example is in Cyril Jolly's biography
of Henry Blogg. Here the object is to present the photographs in as logical
a sequence as possible considering the 84 years that have passed since the
action took place between about noon and 4 pm on 13th December 1933.

55   *Sepoy* has reached a point off the Doctor's Steps breakwater; on the beach the No. 2 lifeboat *Alexandra* is ready to be launched and, on the right, a puff of smoke shows where a rocket is being launched by the Life Saving Brigade.

56   A rocket in flight with its line shrouded in the smoke. One of the crew is on the ratlines.

57   Another rocket being fired. *Sepoy* has drifted slightly further west.

58   Both the crew are clearly visible on the rigging as *Alexandra* tries to reach the barge. Unfortunately, the boat has fouled the rocket line, the tail block of which can be seen in the surf.

59   A while later and *Sepoy* had sunk. *H.F.Bailey*, the second Cromer lifeboat of that name, arrived and is here shown, in one of H.H.Tansley's photographs, trying to get alongside.

60   Another attempt. From a slightly different angle the crew in the rigging cannot be seen against the mast and sail – this applies to all the remaining photos – but they were still there.

61   In this view, the rocket line which had been successfully received on board and hoisted up the mast can be seen. No attempt was made to use it, probably because the men were in no fit state to try and, fortunately, the lifeboat had arrived.

62   *H.F.Bailey* being swept away from *Sepoy* by one of the huge seas.

63 Approaching for another try. This is another of Mr. Tansley's photos.

64 This is probably one of the two successful occasions when the lifeboat was driven onto the wreck and one of the men grabbed from the rigging. Note that here the boat is aft of the rigging to which the crew were clinging. Photo probably by Tansley.

65 And this was the other attempt, this time with the lifeboat on the deck forward of the ratlines.

66 After the action the crowd begins to disperse and *Sepoy* will be left to the night and the sea.

67 Henry Blogg's decision to beach the boat after the *Sepoy* rescue was
the only realistic option. The rescued men needed medical attention
and treatment as soon as possible and this was the first consideration.
The lifeboat could not have been re-housed with the tremendous seas
running, the crew was exhausted after being at sea since 4.30am,
the boat was short of fuel and a further trip to Yarmouth in the
conditions prevailing, and with night coming on, would have been
unthinkable. This photograph was taken the next day, 14th December.
Left to right, the crew present are Henry Blogg; Walter (Primo) Allen,
signalman; H.W. (Swank) Davies, engineer; Jimmy Davies; George
(Buckram) Balls, 2nd coxswain; William J. (Pimpo) Davies; Lewis
(Tuna) Harrison; Jack Davies, bowman; William (Captain) Davies,
2nd engineer; Robert (Skinback) Cox and Charlie Cox. Sydney (Kelly)
Harrison and 'Little Joe' Davies, who were also in the crew the
previous day, were not available for the photo.

68 The remains of the *Sepoy* a few days later. There seems to be no clear record of proceedings from 14th onwards regarding the wreck and its removal. Part of the side of the hull was cut away to allow the removal of the cargo.

69 Captain Joseph Hemstead, *Sepoy*'s skipper, on the beach with Lloyd's agent and Cdr.Harrison, Cromer Secretary of the Shipwrecked Mariners' Association.

70 No mean undertaking. In the first place it must have taken hours to remove the tiles from the wreck and to stack them on the promenade, as shown here. Questions with seemingly no answers arise – how and when were they removed (it would have needed many lorry loads to shift that lot up the Gangway) and were they taken to their intended destination by rail?

71 Henry Blogg standing alongside the tiles. With him is his other award from the *Monte Nevoso* rescue. The captain of that ship presented the dog, which was on board and rescued with the crew, to Henry after it had served six months quarantine. As is well known, he was given the name Monte.

72 At the foot of the Gangway, Henry Blogg preparing bait for crabbing in May 1934.

73 Another shot with Monte watching proceedings.

74 A superb photograph of 'man with broom'. Of a similar date, this shot shows well the granite setts forming the road surface of the Gangway. Beyond the railing is the front of the No. 2 Lifeboat House.

75 In a field on the Norwich Road, Henry has the starting pistol aloft for the Fishermen's Derby at the 1936 Gymkhana.

76   *H.F.Bailey,* the third Cromer lifeboat of that name, being launched
into a gale force north westerly on 10th February 1938. Two fishing
boats were still at sea when the weather deteriorated and the lifeboat
went to search for them. She found the *Urgent* beyond Overstrand and
stood by while that boat was safely beached there. The other boat had
already made it ashore.

77   On board *H.F.Bailey* in 1940 with, left to right, H.T.Davies (Shrimp),
Frank Davies and Henry Blogg. Note the lettering LIFE-BOAT across
the cabin roof for recognition from the air.

78 –80 This photograph of Henry Blogg, which he regarded as his favourite
shot of himself, was one of three taken at the same time on the pier, on
18th March 1940.

81   At an unknown date, probably during the 1920s, the Coastguard
     station was moved to a new position on the top of the west cliff. Prior
     to the outbreak of war in 1939 the Observer Corps, which had come
     into existence in October 1925, opened a post on the station's roof. It is
     shown here in operation just before the war. Mr Bolam and Mr Parker
     are on duty using the plotting instrument to determine the altitude
     and bearing of the aircraft under observation. This information was
     sent by telephone to the Observer Group Centre where it would be
     coordinated with observations from other posts in the area and told
     to the Group Operations Room which, in turn, would pass the details
     to the Fighter Group and Sector Operations Rooms. (This Cromer
     post was possibly designated as Q1 but there is some doubt about
     this). There was, however, no doubt about the vital contribution of
     this volunteer service in the conduct of the air defences of Britain,
     especially in 1940. This was recognized by the award of the prefix
     'Royal' in 1941.

82   The very existence of this Cromer building and its well-tended lawn
     seems today to have been forgotten. It was in the Warren Woods
     and in the 1930s was known as the Tea Garden. In the 1950s it was
     simply referred to as a café. It was possibly too hidden away to attract
     sufficient custom and faded away, almost unnoticed in the late 1950s.

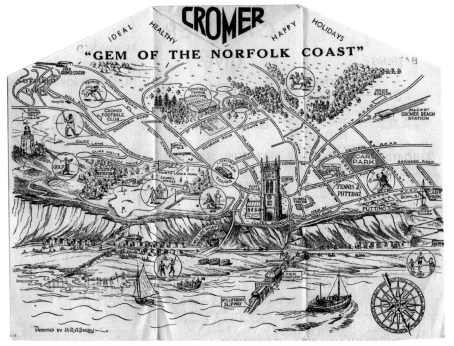

83 A charming period-piece is this publicity leaflet, produced probably shortly after the Second World War, when Cromer was trying to get on its feet again. Note that the Beach Station is still referred to as belonging to the M&GN Railway. Although operation of the M&GN system was wholly taken over by the LNER in October 1936, the old name died hard.

84 & 85   Rough seas at Cromer are not unusual but they do provide an opportunity for dramatic photographs. This pair is of the 'Great North West Gale' of 1ˢᵗ March 1949. No more need be said.

86   The Souvenir Programme of events to mark the Coronation of Her Majesty Queen Elizabeth II. Items listed include a United Coronation Service; A Masque of Famous Women by the Women's Institute; A Grand Carnival Procession on Coronation Day; Teas for the old and young; dances and community singing; bowls, tennis and gymnastic events. And, not least, the town would be honoured with a visit by HMS *Cheerful*.

87   An invitation to a cocktail party which was to turn into an adventure. All was well when the group of those invited was picked up by the ship's motor boat from the steps on the lifeboat slipway and taken out to go aboard. However, while the jollities were under way there was a deterioration in the weather, bringing a strong wind and rough seas. When the time came to return ashore the sea state was such that it was not possible to make a landing on the slipway and the ship's boat could not make a beach landing. There was no alternative but to stay on board overnight and see how conditions were the next morning. The ship's officers made their cabins available to the unexpected guests and the galley went to work to feed the extra mouths (provided, of course, that anyone had an appetite with the ship's movement in that sea!). However, two of the guests were concerned about the well-being of a two-month old son left at home with relations. It was thought that the party would be over in a couple of hours but now the question of feeding the infant loomed large, added to the fact that the baby-sitters would be wondering what had happened. A solution was found in typically practical Royal Navy fashion. Radio contact was made by the ship with Cromer Coastguards who were asked to telephone the baby-sitters to explain the situation and to pass on the all-important recipe for the baby's feed. This was done without difficulty and all was well for the present. Next morning the sea was still rough and there were discussions on how best to get the people ashore. The answer arrived at was the lifeboat. Not, however, the No. 1 lifeboat since, if launched, it would still be impossible to land on the pier and the boat could not be rehoused. That would mean a trip to Yarmouth which was out because of the time it would take and the possible requirement for the boat to be available for an emergency. So the No. 2 lifeboat was launched.

88–90 One of HMS *Cheerful*'s officers took photographs of the pick-up. The first shot shows the lifeboat *Harriot Dixon* manoeuvring to come alongside. In the second, willing hands reach out to assist one of the ladies in the leap onto the lifeboat and in the third, with all the party safely transferred, the lifeboat heads for the beach.

91 Here the boat has come ashore and is being readied for recovery to her carriage. HMS *Cheerful* can be seen on the horizon. A couple of weeks later, *Cheerful* was anchored at Spithead, opposite the entrance to Portsmouth harbour, for the Coronation Review of the Fleet by HM The Queen. But Cromer mourned the loss of two members of *Harriot Dixon*'s crew. In a tragic accident, the crab boat *Boy Jimmy* was swamped close to the shore while coming in from fishing. The lifeboat's coxswain, J.W. (Jimmy) Davies and his brother Frank, together with Ted Bussey, were drowned.

92 A group of crab boats at the foot of the Gangway c.1959. On the
left is YH165 *Black Beauty* and nearest is YH171. Prominent
in the background is Marine View (formerly Beach House)
with its shops on the Promenade including the Poppyland Tea
Rooms. The Red Lion is above and Edinburgh House to the right.

93   Another view with the same boats and this time we have the Lifeboat
House in the background. Also shown is the Pier Theatre with its
postwar extension between the pavilion and the boathouse.

94   In the late summer of 1959 a Metro-Cammell lightweight DMU arrives at Melton Constable off the Cromer and Sheringham line. By this time this was the last section of the former M&GN system to carry a passenger service, being operated as an extension of the old GER Norwich Thorpe to Cromer route. The DMUs kept running until the baleful effects of Dr. Beeching's reshaping saw the Melton to Sheringham section closed on 4th April l964. The DMU in this illustration has the so-called 'speed whiskers' or 'plumes' on the front, the first attempt at a visual warning of approach for men working on the permanent way.

95   A multiple unit passes through the cutting approaching Cromer Beach station, coming in from Sheringham on 29th May 1967.

96   A couple of months earlier, on 20th March 1967, a Metro-Cammell
      lightweight arrives, with the destination blind indicating NORWICH.
      Just above, and to the left of the left hand buffer can be seen a small
      yellow diamond. This was a code to remind staff that the early-built
      units could not be coupled up with the later production DMUs which
      had a blue square code. This was because the multiple unit couplings
      were not compatible between the two groups. All yellow diamond
      units were withdrawn and scrapped by the end of 1969.

97   This is the same train, just stopped, and with a fair number of
      passengers waiting to board. As well as the station buildings with
      their attached platform canopy we have a good view of the BR Eastern
      Region dark blue enamel running-in board bearing the station name.
      Note to the left the line of coal wagons which, at that time, still
      brought in Cromer's domestic coal supplies. (In later years, after all
      the rails in the goods yard had been removed, coal was brought to this
      same site by road. Such was progress).

98   In the later 1960s, the Norwich to Sheringham line was under threat of closure, as the notice board shows in the winter snows of 12th January 1968. That it did not close was in no small part due to the economic advantages of the diesel multiple unit operated service. This was one of the main reasons for their introduction on many routes throughout Britain from the mid-1950s.

99   One of the lightweights coming into Cromer is shown here in the new BR blue livery with a large yellow warning panel beneath the cab windows (but not yet the full yellow end). Also taken on 20th March, 1967, this photo gives a good view of the east side of the gasworks showing the on-site houses provided for the works manager and staff.

100 The lifeboat *Henry Blogg* (ex *Millie Walton*) at sea for an exercise
on 11th April 1964. Here winching practice with a helicopter from
RAF Coltishall is being carried out. XJ723 was a Westland Whirlwind
HAR.10 of the detachment based at Coltishall which was from No 228
Squadron, whose headquarters was at RAF Leconfield, Yorkshire. At
the end of August 1964 the Coltishall unit became D Flight of No 202
Squadron when 228 was officially disbanded and renumbered. The
latter squadron was first formed in Norfolk when, in August 1918, the
flying boat flights at Great Yarmouth Naval Air Station were grouped
into No 228 Squadron of the recently formed Royal Air Force. Since
the 1964 disbandment the squadron has never been re-formed.

101 *Ruby and Arthur Reed* being launched on 18ᵗʰ March 1967. This was not a call-out. The boat had only arrived at Cromer four days before but, after a practice launch that day, she had received damage to a propeller and the port bilge keel while recovering to the slipway. So she was off to Lowestoft for repairs.

102 & 103 The most recent four year civil engineering project to strengthen and repair Cromer's sea defences was completed in 2016. However, work of this sort has been done on many occasions in the past and one example is that shown here. These two views of the rebuilding work on the East Promenade sea wall were taken on 4ᵗʰ May 1975.

104   12th January 1978 and another gale.

105 On a gloomy 12th October 1982 with the south cone hoisted, the lightship relief helicopter prepares to make another trip. The cargo bay is being loaded on the MBB Bo 105 G-BGWP of Management Aviation, under charter to Trinity House. Cromer lighthouse helipad was first used for helicopter flights to lightships on 5th April 1977 when crew changes were made to and from the Dudgeon and Newarp stations. Smiths Knoll and Haisbro were relieved a week later and, from May 1977, Dowsing and Humber were added. Each five-man lightship crew operated a rota of 28 days on/28 days off duty. The helicopter's cabin could accommodate only five persons, including the pilot, necessitating two flights to each vessel to change the crew. In the 1980s a 14-day cycle was introduced, requiring one flight each time in which partial exchanges of the crew were made. Before Cromer helipad was inaugurated, flights were made from the North Denes airfield at Great Yarmouth. This continued to be used and the schedule alternated between the two sites during the remaining years of operation of manned lightships in the southern North Sea.

106 & 107

In the privatised railway era, many operator's colours have come and gone. On the local line, during Anglia days, one of the DMUs, Class 150/2 number 150255 carried the name *Henry Blogg* and a pair of brushed aluminium nameplates bearing a portrait of the great man. The latter was executed somewhat eccentrically, rather like a coarse-screen newspaper reproduction! The date of the photos is 19th March 2004 – in the next year, the new franchise holder disposed of the Class 150s and they were transferred to Wales, presumably without the nameplates.

108 A 1930s winter view in Northrepps Avenue.

109   In the First World War, north Norfolk was considered to be a prime area for a landing by German forces. Consequently, moves were made to provide defences, amongst which were a number of pill-boxes built from concrete blocks. These were positioned at various points on a line between Weybourne and Sea Palling, through North Walsham. Deep water close to the shore made Weybourne particularly vulnerable to attack. The cliffs from there eastwards would deter a frontal assault but the area would need protection against an attack from inland. This pair of pill-boxes was to the east of Metton, guarding a road junction (Ordnance Survey map ref: TG205377) and they were photographed in 1919. It is believed that they were demolished before the advent of the Second World War.

110 & 111   Edwardian ladies' country wear for a winter walk, modelled by Dolly (light coat) and Biddy Gower. The photographs were taken by A.J.Rogers (note the monogram written on the negatives before printing) who operated in, and from, the studio at the top of Balcony House on the corner of Mount Street and Church Street (south side). The sisters worked there as photographer's assistants doing retouching and tinting and, as here, modelling. The location was on the Felbrigg Road, off Hall Road, and the date, conveniently indicated, was March 1909.

112   The tree in the previous photographs is the one left of centre, furthest from the camera in this view taken in the 1930s. This group of three trees was a well-known feature of the local area and made a subject for watercolour artists when seen from the road side. The trees were over-mature pollarded beeches, probably more than 200 years old. Pollarding consisted of cutting the top off a newly mature young tree about six feet above ground level. The result of this was a mass of small branches which were lopped every few years as a source of firewood and to provide fresh browse for cattle. When it became no longer necessary to collect the shoots, the strongest gradually developed into large branches and formed trees with short trunks and broad canopies.

113   (*Top right*) By 1974 only two of these beeches remained. The one featured in.J.Rogers' photographs had fallen twenty or more years earlier. The two here had lost several of their branches and were themselves felled in the 1980s.

114 Characteristic of country Norfolk are the 119 churches with round
towers, several of which adorn the villages which lie to the south-west
of Cromer. As a representative, Sustead is shown here, photographed
on 16th April 1967.

115 A peaceful scene and another country delight, 'The Chequers' public house at Gresham on 9th May 1979. Just out of shot to the left in this picture is the site of Gresham Castle, once a property belonging to the Paston family. It features prominently in the family letters which have survived from the fifteenth century. Dramatic events occurred here in January 1449 when Margaret Paston and her children were evicted in an assault by men of Lord Moleyns, who had a dubious claim to ownership. They sought shelter with close friends in nearby Sustead. (The whole complicated story is well told, amongst much else, in the book 'Blood & Roses' by Helen Castor, Faber & Faber 2004). Who remembers that, in the 1972 Local Government reorganisation, the area which came under the control of the North Norfolk District Council was originally to have been called Pastonacres?

Index